Trailblazer BIOS

SCIENCE EDUCATOR
AND ADVOCATE
BILL NYE

Lerner Publications Company
A division of Lerner Publishing Group, Inc.
241 First Avenue North
Minneapolis, MN USA 55401

For reading levels and more information, look up this title at www.lernerbooks.com.

Library of Congress Cataloging-in-Publication Data
Names: Schwartz, Heather E.
Title: Science educator and advocate Bill Nye / by Heather E. Schwartz.
Description: Minneapolis : Lerner Publications, [2018] | Series: STEM trailblazer bios | Audience: Age 7–11. | Audience: Grade 4 to 6. | Includes bibliographical references and index.
Identifiers: LCCN 2017014150 (print) | LCCN 2017019004 (ebook) | ISBN 9781512499841 (eb pdf) | ISBN 9781512499810 (lb : alk. paper)
Subjects: LCSH: Nye, Bill. | Science television programs—Juvenile literature. | Science in mass media—Juvenile literature. | Mechanical engineers—United States—Biography—Juvenile literature.
Classification: LCC Q225 (print) | LCC Q225 .S227 2018 (ebook) | DDC 509.2 [B]—dc23

LC record available at https://lccn.loc.gov/2017014150

Manufactured in the United States of America
1-43617-33368-6/7/2017

The images in this book are used with the permission of: WENN Ltd/Alamy Stock Photo, p. 4; © PBS/Courtesy Everett Collection, pp. 5, 12; Seth Poppel Yearbook Library, p. 6; © Meutia Chaerani/Wikimedia Commons (CC BY-SA 3.0), p. 8; Beitia Archives Digital Press Photos/Newscom, p. 9; Everett Collection Inc/Alamy Stock Photo, p. 10; Scott J. Ferrell/Congressional Quarterly/Alamy Stock Photo, p. 13; AP Photo/Mark Lennihan, p. 15; © Planet Green/Courtesy Everett Collection, p. 16; NASA/JPL-Caltech/Cornell, p. 17; NASA/JPL-Caltech, p. 18; © Don DeBold/flickr.com (CC BY 2.0), p. 21; B Christopher/Alamy Stock Photo, p. 22; bibiphoto/Shutterstock.com, p. 23; chaiviewfinder/Shutterstock.com, p. 24; Anthony Behar/Sipa USA/Newscom, p. 25; AP Photo/Louie Balukoff, p. 26; © Paul Fenton/ZUMA Wire/Alamy Stock Photo, p. 27.

Front cover: Everett Collection/Newscom.

Main body text set in Adrianna Regular 13/22. Typeface provided by Chank.

CONTENTS

Chapter 1

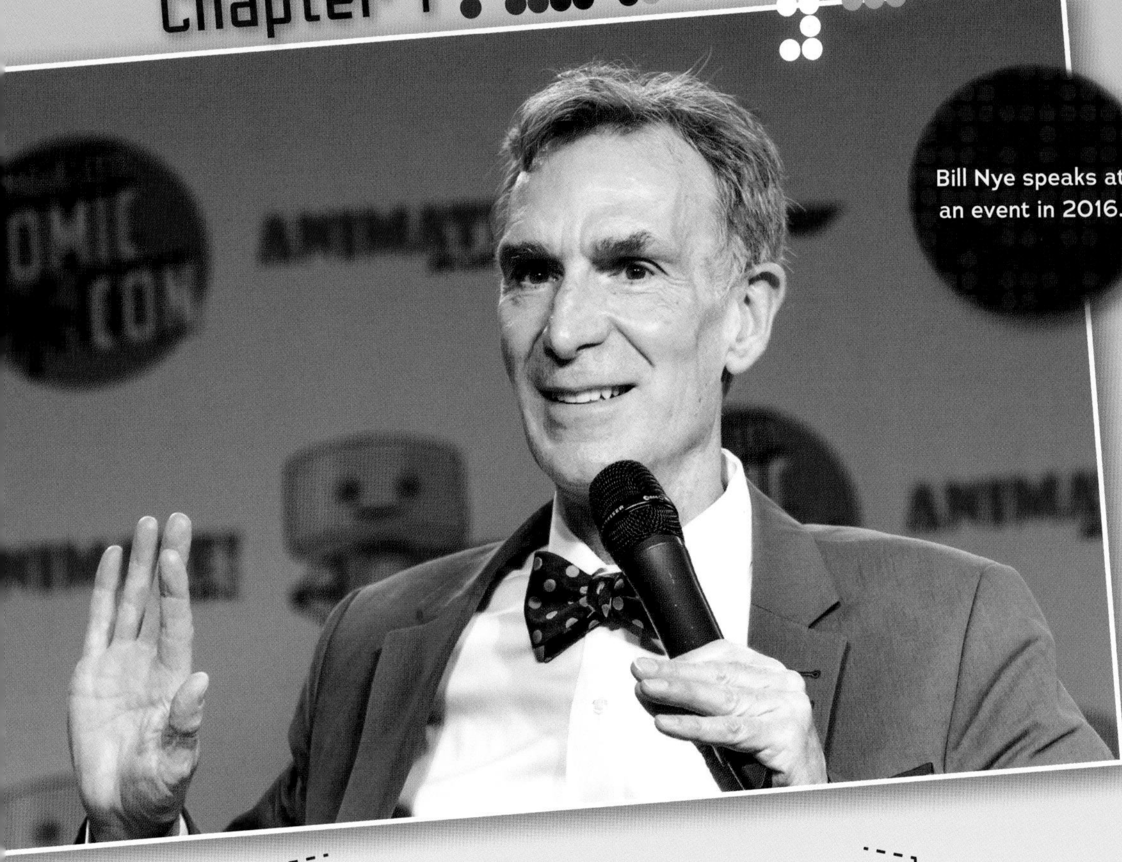

Bill Nye speaks at an event in 2016.

EARLY INTERESTS

William (Bill) Sanford Nye has always loved science. As a kid, he was fascinated by bees. He also thought bicycles and airplanes were cool. He knew that one day he wanted to become a **mechanical engineer**.

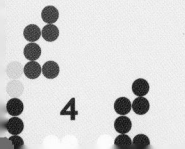

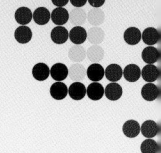

But Nye's professional life was not all about science. He started doing stand-up comedy. Then he found a unique way to combine his passions for science and comedy. He went on TV to teach kids and to dig into his life's work: saving the world through science.

Nye went on to become the host of a popular kids' TV show in the 1990s.

SCIENCE FROM THE START

Bill was born on November 27, 1955. His parents were both interested in math and science. His mother, Jacqueline, had worked as a code breaker during World War II (1939–1945). His father, Edwin, had a scientific mind and always encouraged Bill to make things. His father was also fascinated by sundials. He'd spent four years without electricity as a prisoner of war in Japan. There he'd learned to tell time by watching the shadow of a shovel handle as it moved and changed throughout the day. Growing up in Washington, DC, Bill learned all about sundials from his dad.

   Bill went to public elementary school. But his parents worked hard to get him into a private high school because they believed he would get a better education there. Bill worked hard too. He earned a partial scholarship to attend Sidwell Friends School. His teachers encouraged his interests in science and math.

Bill poses for a photo during his senior year of high school.

After graduating from Sidwell Friends School in 1973, Bill went to Cornell University in Ithaca, New York. He studied mechanical engineering. He also took an **astronomy** class taught by the famous scientist Carl Sagan. Bill was impressed by Sagan's lectures. He has continued to be inspired by Sagan's words throughout his career.

TECH TALK

"When you listened to Carl Sagan talk or lecture, he was eloquent. He used perfectly chosen words that were inspirational. Everything he talked about had this wonderful quality to it, this reverence for the cosmos and our place within it."

—*Bill Nye*

Chapter 2

A Boeing factory in Seattle, Washington

CREATING HIS CAREER

After graduating from Cornell, Nye went to work as a mechanical engineer for Boeing in Seattle, Washington. The company designs and sells airplanes and spacecraft. Nye developed a hydraulic pressure resonance suppressor tube for a 747 airplane. The tube decreased vibrations in the steering mechanism. The design took him three years to complete.

While working at Boeing, Nye heard about a contest to find someone who looked like the comedian Steve Martin. A friend in college had told Nye he looked like the comedian, so Nye decided to enter. He won a local round of the contest in Seattle!

Steve Martin is a popular comedian, actor, and writer.

ASPIRING ASTRONAUT

Throughout his career, Nye wanted to be an astronaut and travel into space. He wanted to see the world in a different way so he could work to change it. Nye applied to the astronaut program at the National Aeronautics and Space Administration (NASA) many times but was always rejected. One reason may have been that he did not have a PhD.

THE COMEDY GUY

Nye did not go on to win the national contest. But he found a way to expand on his local victory. People asked Nye to act like Steve Martin at parties. He developed his own comedy material too.

Nye continues to be passionate about both entertaining and helping people.

For about seven years, Nye kept his job as an engineer and pursued his hobby as a stand-up comic on the side. He enjoyed making people laugh. Nye also saw a link between science and comedy. Both were about giving to people. As an engineer, Nye created things that made people's lives easier. As a comedian, he improved people's lives by making them feel better.

In 1986, Nye's career took a sharp turn toward comedy. He was asked to join the cast of a Seattle comedy show called *Almost Live!* Nye quit his Boeing job and became a comedy writer and performer. But he wasn't really leaving science behind.

TECH TALK

"When you look into my eyes, you believe me because I'm passionate about it. It's very interesting to me. There's nothing cooler than science."

—*Bill Nye*

Chapter 3

Nye became Bill Nye the Science Guy in 1993.

THE
SCIENCE GUY

One day Nye learned during a writers' meeting that an episode of *Almost Live!* was going to be short by six minutes. They needed something to fill the extra time. So the host suggested that Nye take those minutes to teach science. He said Nye could be "Bill Nye the Science Guy."

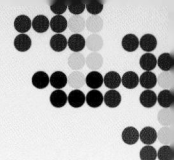

Nye loved the idea. Suddenly, he had a catchy new nickname that described his mission and his personality perfectly. By 1993, Nye had his own show on Seattle's PBS station. It was called *Bill Nye the Science Guy.*

STARRING BILL NYE

Nye's goal for his show was ambitious. He wanted to change the world. He wanted to teach kids about science and inspire future scientists. He covered all kinds of scientific topics on

his show. His topics were serious, but he made the show fun and funny. He made science exciting for kids.

Nye used props and demonstrations to teach viewers about science concepts.

MAKING MUSIC

Music writer Mike Greene, a former math teacher, wrote the "Bill Nye the Science Guy" theme song. He wanted the music and lyrics to be edgy. The song had to open a show that was more grown-up than other kids' shows. Professional rappers chanted Nye's name, and Greene sang other parts of the song himself. He wanted to hire singers, but the show's producers thought Greene's voice was funnier.

The show began with a catchy song that included a chant of Nye's name. Viewers loved the song. The lyrics included the science fact, "Inertia is a property of matter." This means that matter will stay as it is until something forces it to change. Nye's show was unique because it could teach those kinds of difficult ideas to kids.

In an episode about heat, Nye used a blowtorch to melt ice into water. In an episode about insects, he explained that an **exoskeleton** is made of material similar to human fingernails. The show was filled with jokes, skits, experiments, and songs—

all about science. Nye's delivery was never boring. He wasn't afraid to be goofy to get his point across.

Nye's approach was successful and popular. His show ran for five seasons, from 1993 to 1998. It won nineteen Emmy awards. More important, it inspired young people to get excited about science.

Nye holds his 1998 Emmy award.

TECH TALK

"There's nothing I believe in more strongly than getting young people interested in science and engineering for a better tomorrow, for all humankind."

—*Bill Nye*

Chapter 4

Nye on the 2008 show *Stuff Happens*

STILL
A SCIENTIST

When Nye's show ended, he worked on several other TV shows, some for older viewers. He wrote children's books about science. He also made special appearances in movies and videos. After all, he was a celebrity.

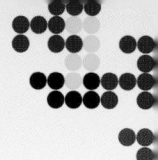

But Nye was still a scientist. He used his fame to spread information about science. He also kept up his scientific work.

SUNDIALS IN SPACE

In 2000, Nye was invited to a meeting about NASA's Mars Exploration Rover mission. NASA was planning to send rovers to Mars to explore the planet. Nye decided he wanted to create sundials that could go to Mars with these robotic vehicles.

This image of the Mars Rover *Spirit* and the surface of Mars was taken by cameras on *Spirit*.

The black rod on the MarsDial casts a shadow to help scientists tell time on Mars.

On Earth, a sundial is a flat round surface marked with the hours of the day. The shadow cast by the sun shows what time it is by the mark it lands on. Nye's MarsDial worked in the same way. Unlike regular sundials, however, MarsDials did not stay in one place. They moved around on the rovers. That meant permanent hour marks on the MarsDial wouldn't be accurate.

The team that designed the MarsDials left them blank instead. In photos of the MarsDials, they added hour marks electronically to tell the time accurately.

The rovers already had other clocks. But the MarsDials served another purpose too. MarsDials helped scientists figure out how to adjust cameras on the rover from Earth. That way, they could get the best, most accurate pictures of colors on Mars.

Two identical MarsDials were placed on two Mars rovers named *Spirit* and *Opportunity*. The MarsDials are each only about 3 inches (7.6 cm) square, and they are each inscribed with the motto Two Worlds, One Sun, and the name Mars in seventeen different languages. Nye suggested including

TECH TALK

"People launched this spacecraft from Earth in our year 2003. It arrived on Mars in 2004. We built its instruments to study the Martian environment and to look for signs of life. We used this post and these patterns to adjust our cameras and as a sundial to reckon the passage of time. The drawings and words represent the people of Earth. We sent this craft in peace to learn about Mars' past and about our future. To those who visit here, we wish a safe journey and the joy of discovery."

—*MarsDials* inscription

these inscriptions. He was excited about the idea of sending a message into space, to future explorers of Mars.

CONTINUING TO CONTRIBUTE

In 2005, Nye became vice president of the Planetary Society. In 2010, he became the chief executive officer. Nye said he was honored to take a leadership role in an organization founded by his former professor Carl Sagan.

Nye opened a Climate Lab at the Chabot Space and Science Center in Oakland, California, in 2010. His goal for the lab was to teach children about climate change. The lab was fun, like his shows. It included several interactive displays. Kids could learn about energy by pulling a lever to operate a windmill. They could also operate a wave machine to power a miniature lighthouse.

INFLUENTIAL PROFESSOR

Carl Sagan worked with NASA. He was famous for focusing on the search for extraterrestrial life. He wrote several books about astronomy. And in 1980, he cofounded the Planetary Society, an organization focused on space exploration.

Bill Nye's Climate Lab is filled with fun interactive exhibits.

Nye said the lab was meant for ten-year-olds. He believes that children who are excited about science by the age of ten will continue to be excited about science throughout their lives. At a preview of the Climate Lab, Nye noted that every adult there had been ten once too. He was excited to continue teaching children as well as adults about science.

Chapter 5

Nye speaks about climate change at a 2016 conference.

SAVING
THE WORLD

Nye's decision to develop a Climate Lab was not random. He was serious when it came to educating the public about scientific issues such as climate change. He spoke out when he felt people did not understand scientific facts.

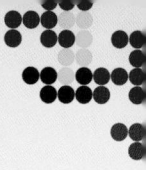

CHALLENGING MYTHS

Nye used his knowledge and celebrity to publicly take on people who did not believe climate change is a serious problem. One major effect of climate change is an increase in Earth's temperature. Scientists say humans are causing Earth to warm up too quickly. Humans release too much **carbon dioxide** into the **atmosphere**. Carbon dioxide comes from things people use such as power plants, cars, and planes.

Traffic is a major source of carbon dioxide in the atmosphere.

Nye talked to the media and posted videos online explaining the science behind climate change. He explained that the change in Earth's temperature over the past century sounds very small, but science shows that this change matters. Nye said that 97 percent of climate scientists believe humans are causing climate change. Nye urged people not to waste energy and to use energy sources that do not release carbon dioxide. Wind turbines and solar panels, for example, create power by using energy from the wind and the sun.

Wind turbines turn energy from the wind into electricity.

Nye speaks at a 2016 event about social issues.

TECH TALK

"You have to be optimistic. You have to believe you can solve these problems or you will not solve them. So let's go, everybody, let's save the world."

—*Bill Nye*

Nye speaks to a crowd at an environmental rally in 2000.

Nye also challenged people who do not believe humans **evolved** from **primates**. These people often also believe Earth is less than ten thousand years old. They do not want children to learn about evolution in school.

Nye's fame gives him many opportunities to speak out about the causes he believes in.

In 2012, Nye posted a video online explaining the importance of teaching evolution. He said that dinosaur bones and distant stars tell us Earth is billions of years old. Nye's video quickly got more than one million views.

ALWAYS AN EDUCATOR

In 2017, Nye released a new Netflix show called *Bill Nye Saves the World*. It features science experiments, special guests, and celebrity appearances. But the main goal of the show is in the title. Nye wants to save the world. He wants to expose myths about science. And he wants to educate people and help bring up a generation of children who understand science.

For Nye, science is always about more than facts. It is about putting facts into action. Nye has never stopped working to bring science to other people—especially children who could use science to create a better world.

TIMELINE

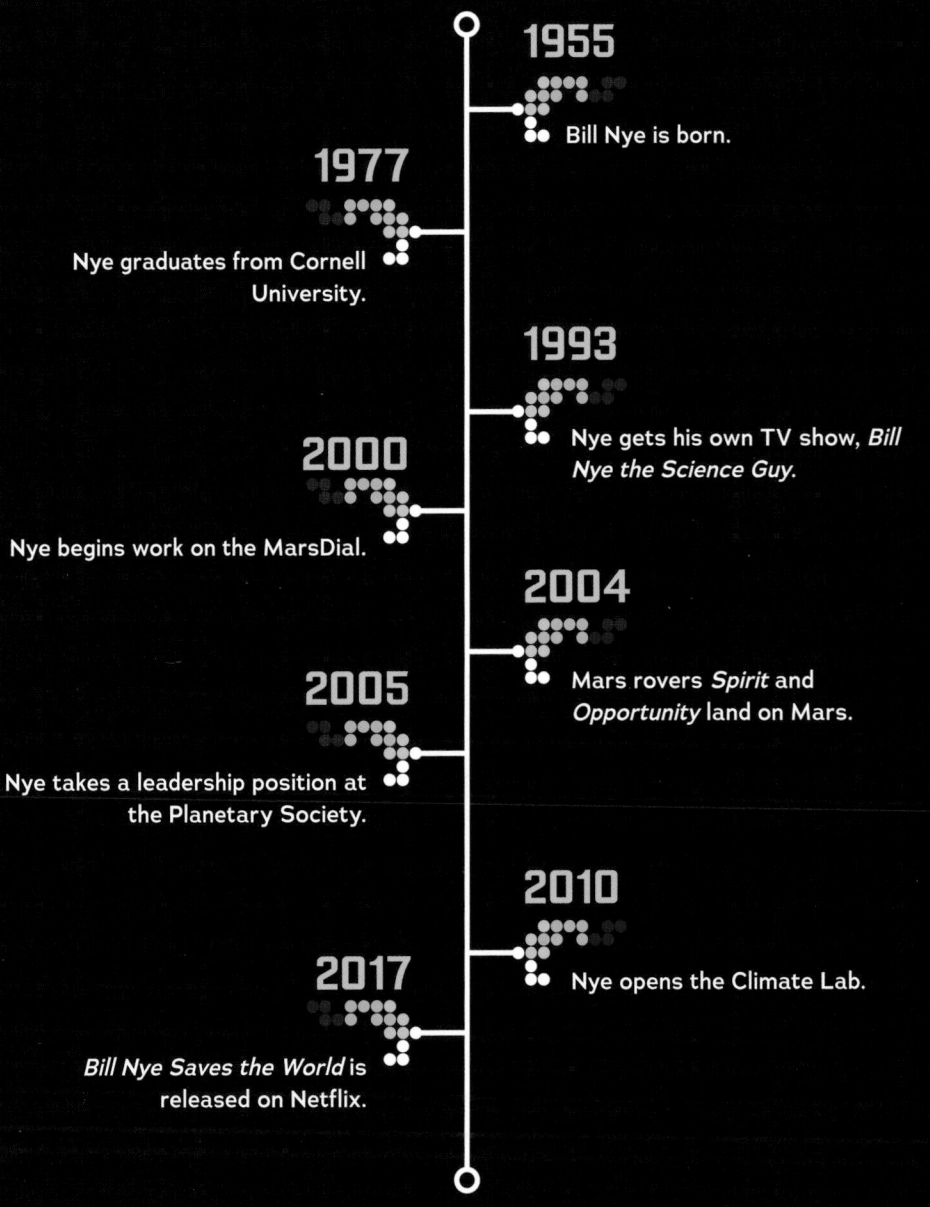

1955
Bill Nye is born.

1977
Nye graduates from Cornell University.

1993
Nye gets his own TV show, *Bill Nye the Science Guy*.

2000
Nye begins work on the MarsDial.

2004
Mars rovers *Spirit* and *Opportunity* land on Mars.

2005
Nye takes a leadership position at the Planetary Society.

2010
Nye opens the Climate Lab.

2017
Bill Nye Saves the World is released on Netflix.

SOURCE NOTES

7 "Bill Talks about How Carl Sagan Changed His Life," CornellCast, August 20, 2015, http://www.cornell.edu/video/bill-nye-carl-sagan-connection.

11 Pamela Davis, "Bill Nye, the Successful Guy," *St. Petersburg Times*, October 11, 1999, https://web.archive.org/web/20080305115010/http://www.sptimes.com/News/101199/news_pf/Floridian/Bill_Nye_the_success.shtml.

15 John Schwartz, "Firebrand for Science, and Big Man on Campus: On TV and the Lecture Circuit, Bill Nye Aims to Change the World," *New York Times*, June 17, 2013, http://www.nytimes.com/2013/06/18/science/bill-nye-firebrand-for-science-is-a-big-man-on-campus.html.

19 David Brand, "Bill Nye's 'Cool' Interplanetary Sundial Heads for Mars as a Calibration Tool—and a Magnet for Schoolchildren," *Cornell Chronicle*, December 23, 2003, http://www.news.cornell.edu/stories/2003/12/bill-nyes-cool-interplanetary-sundial-heads-mars.

25 Melissa Gaskill, "What Bill Nye Wishes We All Would Do about Climate Change," *Men's Journal*, accessed April 21, 2017, http://www.mensjournal.com/entertainment/articles/what-bill-nye-wishes-we-all-would-do-about-climate-change-w213017.

GLOSSARY

astronomy
the scientific study of objects in outer space

atmosphere
the whole mass of air surrounding Earth

carbon dioxide
a gas produced when people and animals breathe out or when certain fuels are burned. Carbon dioxide is used by plants for energy.

evolved
changed or developed gradually

exoskeleton
a rigid external covering on the body

mechanical engineer
a type of engineer concerned with the use of machines

primates
any member of the group of animals that includes apes and monkeys

FURTHER INFORMATION

BOOKS

Green, Dan. *Climate Change: A Hot Topic!* New York: Kingfisher, 2015.
Read more about the science behind climate change.

Nye, Bill, and Gregory Mone. *At the Bottom of the World.* New York: Amulet Books, 2017.
This is Nye's first book in a fictional series based on scientific facts.

Swanson, Jennifer. *Environmental Activist Wangari Maathai.* Minneapolis: Lerner Publications, 2018.
Learn about another activist who wanted to change the world and fight climate change.

WEBSITES

Bill Nye the Science Guy
http://billnye.com
Check out Nye's latest videos and photos.

Climate Kids
http://climatekids.nasa.gov/climate-change-meaning
Learn about NASA's take on climate change.

Mars for Kids
https://mars.nasa.gov/participate/funzone
Try out these games and activities to learn more about NASA's exploration of Mars.

LERNER

Expand learning beyond the printed book. Download free, complementary educational resources for this book from our website, www.lerneresource.com.

SOURCE

INDEX

ABOUT THE AUTHOR

Heather E. Schwartz has written more than sixty nonfiction books for kids. She always enjoys researching and learning about people with a passion for what they do, like Bill Nye.